Swedish Death Cleaning

Cleaning

Downsize Your Way to a Happy Home and Life

(A Comprehensive and Practical Guide to a Clutter-free Life)

Russel Guthrie

Published By **Region Loviusher**

Russel Guthrie

Swedish Death Cleaning: Downsize Your Way to a Happy Home and Life (A Comprehensive and Practical Guide to a Clutter-free Life)

ISBN   978-1-990373-77-0

Legal & Disclaimer

Table Of Contents

Chapter 1: Swedish Death Cleaning Demystified

What is Swedish Death Cleaning?

Swedish death-cleaning, or dostadning in Swedish it is the practice of clearing your house and personal life while leaving only those items and possessions that provide you with satisfaction. While it's not a brand novel idea, Swedish death cleaning came into the spotlight after Swedish-born author and artist Margareta Magnusson, published her best-selling book, "The Gentle Art of Swedish Death Cleaning: How to Free Yourself and Your Family from a Lifetime of Clutter," that promotes the Scandinavian tradition of cleaning prior to death. The book's publication became a reality the book has seen the emergence of a decluttering movement across the media with more people than ever ready and willing to embrace the notion of clearing out their homes prior to their passing. The notion behind Swedish death-cleaning is distinct from normal cleaning and dusting in the sense that it advises you to get rid of objects that interfere with the flow of your house and lifestyle and only keep those things that you and those around you want to keep. Although it might sound like a lot of effort to get rid of everything that you do not feel a necessity to keep, Margareta Magnusson, in her book, states "Death cleaning means removing unnecessary things and making your home nice and orderly when you think the time is coming close for you to leave the planet." Thus the essence of dying cleaning is the process of removing items that are considered to be junk in your house as you get older.

The notion of Swedish death cleansing is an ancient tradition among the Swedes who, at the middle of their lives start the process of slowly getting rid of belongings which no longer bring joy within their lives. The idea behind it is that if the objects do make you happy as well as the happiness of your family members, the item is not of use so it must be thrown away.

The process of death cleaning isn't just the disposal of things that were a part of the home or in your heart. it's about recognizing the moments or events and the positive memories they've provided, then evaluating objectively whether they have something to contribute or if the more enlightened days are past. Looking back over the time you've spent and expressing gratitude to the possessions that made your lives enjoyable, before taking them off of the task before finally laying them down to rest, or letting them away to keep creating wonderful memories and bonds with others. It is important to remember that in Swedish dying cleaning, you do not "throw" your items away instead, you "lay them to rest" after you have thanked them for their dedication to the cause. De-cluttering your home as well as your daily life is among the most beneficial actions you can take for you and your loved ones, as it not only alleviate you from the burden of having to search through the countless things you use every day, but it also provides you the feeling of fulfillment knowing you'll leave your family without the physical obligation of cleaning up your home once you've no longer with them. The happiness you feel when you die cleaning is far greater than the emotional stress that could result from the process. This is the best "last act" you could give to your family and friends.

Benefits of Death Cleaning

Alongside giving your home an energizing new look and appearance the way you want it to be, here are the advantages of doing a death clean:

The death cleaning program offers instruction in meditation. With ever-changing pressures of living in the present our minds are so with the process of progressing and climbing the corporate ladder to where there isn't the time to concentrate on the most important things in life including the possibility of dying. If you clean your home it is not just about ridding your body of unneeded materials and waste, but you also get closer to the harsh realisation of the fact that you are dying. For those who are older dying clean is an opportunity to come to terms with age and the onset of senility.

This takes that feeling of overwhelm out of your head. There are few things that can be so overwhelming as the clutter that can be found in the home. The problem is more when you are suffering from or are predisposed to being afflicted by a mental disorder because they're more sensitive to the environment as opposed to mentally strong people. The process of death cleaning opens up more room, and usually the more space is a sign of peace.

Cleaning up after death generally increases your joy. Cleaning your home can bring closeness to loved family members and provides an opportunity for you to spend time with them. It can increase the joy of your daily life.

Deciding what you want to wear is no longer an issue after you've passed away in a clean manner. There's no reason to not keep plenty of clothes that you don't have any use for or within your closet. Cleaning out your closet helps eliminate clothes you do not require and helps you store only items of high-quality that are actually used. Your closet is more appealing as crowded and unattractive.

In the course of death cleaning it is possible to find a piece of furniture it's been a while since you have, or may have had to purchase yet again. Additionally, when you die cleaning, you'll be very selective about what you purchase and the things you put away, in worry of not bringing clutter back into the home. It saves cash, time and energy. time.

The Swedish method of dying cleaning helps you respect the items you have, and to view these items as people rather than just objects. If you view your possessions as integral parts of your existence as opposed to disposable, unimportant objects, they become more appealing to your eyes.

After decluttering the house, routine clean-up and dusting are simple and pleasant, since your home will have taken shape and order.

The process of death cleaning generally gives an impression of direction and a sense of focus. As you go through the entire process, you'll be able to see that you have not consciously learned to be a person to be selective. It becomes very clear which foods to consume and what you can buy, the kind of events to host within your house and what ones you can let slip, and which ones to retain and which ones to leave behind. It's a real sense of organization, and everything starts to come together flawlessly.

The best date for the death Cleaning?

Based on the opinions of experts, the ideal time to begin death cleansing is between 50 and 60. It is also possible to start slightly earlier, for instance at the middle of your life.

Chapter 2: The "How": Technique/Method Of Swedish Death Cleaning

The chapter explains how to carry out Swedish death cleansing. This process is reduced into specific steps to facilitate greater comprehension. The steps include:

Be aware of what you're engaging in

The first step in the process. It is important to know the exact nature of what you're undertaking before you begin to explore it. Dostadning is not your typical cleaning. It's much more than just dancing around your home using the aid of a vacuum cleaner or an earful of soulful music playing in the background. there's a lot you can do with the music, however. Dostadning is a method which teaches you how to tidy the entire house so that after your death in the future, the Loved Ones will not have to deal with the burden of removing and cleaning objects they've never used...or perhaps even saw. It's essentially in a way, it is the final comprehensive cleaning tasks that you'll have to undertake before passing away. Also, much more emotional energy is associated with funeral cleaning than any other regular decluttering and cleaning method.

If you've had the chance to think about what's going to happen with all of your clothes, jewelry bags, shoes and other papers after you pass away, you could have figured out the fact that, when you die and die, the care for those items is going to be the sole responsibility of those that you've left to follow. The decision they make to them - throw away or sell them and donate them - it will take their own initiative, determination and resources. If your family members don't wish to dump all the things you've left behind into rubbish, and they'll with reverence and affection for your sacrifice, invest an enormous amount of effort during the process of decluttering in order in order to give a proper justice to your old belongings. It can be very exhausting and stressful. When you start your dying-cleaning process it is in order to keep your life so easy and enjoyable as is possible. Also, you will do your family members a great deal of good, by not wasting the energy that they will later require.

Naturally, the process as well as the idea of tidying out in preparation for your passing may be uncomfortable and gruelling and uncomfortable. However, doing dostadning is the best and most considerate act to take for your as well as your loved ones. The cleanup will be more crucial at the time of your loss of life, there's the possibility your family will require a move into a smaller home. When that occurs you will have a pressing necessity to reduce the size of your home and save only those things you need to keep and the items that keep you and the people you love. One reason that you do not have the option of delaying the death-cleaning process is due to because with time, you will acquire more and more things and you'll require more energy to complete the cleanup and more energy to start it. According to this you should know that the most effective day to get started cleaning was just yesterday. The second most effective day to do it is now. With time, it'll get more challenging to finish it.

Another reason you should get your funeral cleaning completed is that, upon your death family members will have to preserve some objects you have left to them. In the case, for instance, you were given a gold pendant from your mother prior to her passing died and preserved the necklace in a safe place shining up to now what would you do to ensure that your family members be able to share the necklace among themselves? Which one will get the necklace once you're gone? If this happens, it will cause some batting of the eyelids between your kids or in the most extreme cases it could cause anger and even bad blood. It is important to be aware of the possibility of extreme situations particularly if you have children that don't seem to have a great relationship. If you want to avoid unpleasant situations, it is recommended to think about removing your necklace. This could be done by transferring it to someone else before you hand it over either by selling it or giving it away.

Begin with the smallest of things

Naturally, it isn't easy to let go of things that you've had for years, and especially items that you hold a strong connection to, like present from parents or grandparents, keepsakes from special such as weddings, birthdays or baby showers, etc. These things are typically important to us and are a part of our lives. But, how many of them still give you satisfaction? How many will your family members be content to own? Perhaps you believe that something is essential as it is a part of your memory of a particular event, such as the (now obsolete) toy your dad gifted to you at the time you were top of your class at the end of 3rd grade- but in reality that your memory of the moment will remain afloat even without the tangible thing that reminds you the occasion. It will be surprising how little you'd be missing the item in case you had to get rid of it. That's not to minimize the importance of collecting souvenirs or memorabilia. But, if your house is a mess because of the inability to get rid of the old stuff, you might be unable to function with the current.

Swedish funeral cleaning can be odd, strange, or overwhelming, however it's not too unreasonable. If you're finding difficult to get rid of the things you have, begin by removing the smaller items which you'd normally think of as garbage. They include books and papers which have lost their value and are worn out shoes, clothing that are no longer suitable outdated and damaged technology, dusty old toys, as well as sports equipment you do not use. If you're unsure that an product is beneficial to anyone in your household or not then you can invite your entire family (and their own families and particularly your children) over for some look-sees and make a decision for themselves. It's a wonderful occasion to spend time with your loved ones. When you look through your belongings, you can relate stories of them to make connections with your family members while doing it. You may also find things they'll cherish and love by acquiring your belongings. The result is win-win. Engaging your family members to the event will surely help in simplifying the process and making it more entertaining.

For the first step in cleaning begin by locating a place which you can be able to use for a temporary storage area, like the basement or attic, or any combination of the two depending on how much you'd like to get rid of. If you decide to start the process begin with items you are able to throw away in the attic or basement without second thoughts. Do not begin with paper or books because they could weigh your mind and cause you to taking longer than required to do so. There is a possibility to stop reading every letter you've written, or take a look and recall memories about every person on the photo. It's not easy to progress in this manner. Beginning with what you're least emotionally attached to and put aside books, papers and photos for the end.

Most pets that your pet has will automatically be loved and cared for by your family members, which means there may no need to have arrangements for what will happen to them if your death occurs. There are a few instances where an individual has a pet they love but family members don't enjoy. Imagine, for instance, that you have a dog within the family of cats or keeping a parrot even though the majority of the family doesn't like the way it looks or sounds. If your family isn't able to accept your pet following your death, think about moving your pet into an animal home where they'll be well looked after.

Let your loved ones know about the idea of dying and the concept of cleaning

It was considered rude to inquire about parents' wishes on the things they plan to do in the event of their death. It's a relief that the Times are changing. The public is becoming increasingly comfortable discussing their overall health and their mortality. If you have parents who are elderly who may not be starting your death-cleaning routine because of ignorance, lack of motivation or some other cause this is the perfect best time to talk about the issue with your parents. The idea of funeral cleaning in a polite, gentle as well as honest and imaginative manner, in order that they will be inspired to get involved instead of being detached and disengaged. Consider taking this action now, particularly in the event that the task of cleaning after their death will fall on you. For instance, you could asking your parents "What do you plan to do with all of your belongings when you are no longer able to take care of yourself?" The idea should instantly spark ideas about cleaning their heads.

If their reaction doesn't show an eagerness to begin the process of cleaning then you are able to push them further however, with care and prudence. You don't need to rush the process at this stage because it's so that it is easy to see them get frustrated by the question and consequently, abandon the notion of cleaning off forever. It is possible to ask "Would you like us to give away some of these things you no longer need?" or "Do you want me to help you start clearing up some of your items gradually so that it wouldn't become overwhelming for us later on?" If they aren't able to grasp the message you can try playing around with using the same words and changing the words until they are able to comprehend what that you're talking about. Be careful not to be aggressive, threatening or uninformed when you approach them at any the cost. Your goal is to encourage and help them navigate the process, not push them. It's difficult to maintain a sense of respect and courtesy when discussing the subject of funeral cleaning together with loved ones, therefore, ensure that you have the endurance and perseverance to carry it out. An effective way of approaching this topic is with a bit of humorous facts, or you could consider bringing up the custom in the time of Vikings. The Vikings laid their bodies to rest together with their belongings in order that they would not be missing them when they died. Although this may sound like a pity even in the modern world, burial of the deceased with their possessions spared family members of the deceased from from being able to manage their possessions in the future. Create a story that is as amusing and as mellow as is possible and make it easy that they can comprehend the message you want to convey.

Make sure you are mindful of the of the process

It is essential to do death cleaning not just because it's an effective method of cleaning your physical surroundings and also helps to prevent negative emotions from the loved ones of yours when they come into contact with items belonging to you. If you're hiding a particular behaviour or habit, think about what it would be like for a relatives to find things that reveal your hidden. Consider the extent to which your perception of someone would be affected when you learn of a hidden habit they had while living. If you're a victim of unflattering books, documents diaries, or other belongings that might alter the person you love dearly and your family, it is recommended to get your possessions. They should not be kept within your home or in any other place in fact, they must be destroyed completely either by burning them, or feeding them into shredders to totally erase all trace of them.

If you are unable to part with things that you cherish, no matter how devastating the discovery of them by loved family members could be, place them in a garbage container. Label the container "Trash, please throw away" in order that whoever is cleaning the area can dispose of the items by sorting the items. In this way, you don't need burn the items you have stored or put them in shredders. However, there's still the risk of finding its way into the hands of a curious person, it's more beneficial to keep your item as unnoticeable as you can, similar to throwing away the box.

Take Care of Photographs

After you have every other object sorted out Then, pay attention to the things that you've put aside for the the last time: books, papers and photos. Particularly pay attention to photos as they carry lots of feelings. Photos are a significant part of your collection because they are a source of stories and trigger memories. It is recommended that you preserve the majority of your photos because they can help your loved ones after you're gone. It is important to remember, nevertheless, that everyone has distinctive views and places distinct levels of significance with photos. The fact that a picture of your son and you is your first thing to look at every morning, it doesn't mean that the picture is more valuable that a normal snapshot the other. To determine which of your children might be interested in which photograph think about creating the option of a photo album, and then giving them pictures every now and then to let them choose which photos they would like to see as well as which they wouldn't. It's a good method of determining what is important to who.

For making the task of sorting your personal photos easier it is possible to begin by eliminating duplicates of your snapshot. If you have more than identical copies of similar photos Keep one copy and dispose of all the others. After you're finished then move on to the next stage: getting rid of photographs with faces that which you are unable to identify or even name. It's likely that if you don't know the individuals in your photo, nobody will be able to at home. Thus, the photos are not important to save. Digital technology in media has made the process of storing photographs much easier and more efficient. If you own hardcopies of photos, you may save them digitally and easily with a USB storage device. Then, you can eliminate a lot photos that are physically stored. This will not only help you save the space and energy but it also safeguards photos from destruction like when they come into exposure to chemicals or other chemicals.

Protect the future of the data you store online

After clearing out your home and organizing your home You then need be able to concentrate on the web activities. It is possible that you do not wish for your web-based accounts - email accounts, social media profiles cloud services, and even mobile internet services as well as subscriptions to remain in existence even after your departure. Whichever option you choose it is essential that someone take over the task after you're no more in a position to. For this, you must create a note of every one of the information you have on your online forms (usernames or passwords, pins, digital keys.) and also what needs to be done to each account or service (whether to stop them or allow them to continue) Put it carefully in a safe place. In the box, write "My online details" and keep it there. If there is a time of your passing away, your loved ones may contact this box and gain access to your account online and execute your directives.

Leçons to learn from Swedish death cleaning

Here are some essential lessons to be learned from Swedish death-cleaning:

It's not so difficult as you think. The idea of removing clutter not just for the sake of having more living space, but also to make room for the day you die could seem overwhelming. Through the steps and guidelines in the Swedish Death Cleaning Plan We soon discover that it's not nearly quite as difficult as we first thought. Clean-up can be entertaining and fun when you are in an appropriate mindset and enthusiasm, as well as with those who are in the right place. In addition to making your house much less cluttered and busy, death cleaning could create such a tidy environment in your home, that you don't require to hunt for important papers or keys as there will be no more places they could become lost.

The process of cleaning up your death space is not only for you. It's about the people that you have left to follow. Cleaning up after the loss of a loved one is a difficult task or exhausting, even a bit confusing because it is difficult to know what they felt regarding their possessions and what they'd have liked their final fate. Deciding whether to dispose of to others, save, or even recycle can be an overwhelming task. The process of cleaning out your death room encourages you to think beyond asking yourself what makes an item satisfied, but also consider whether its presence will be appreciated by the people you have left behind after passing to. Answering the second one should be taken with the same seriousness as the answer to the one.

Death cleaning is available anytime at any time in your life, regardless of your current level of overall health. Many people believe, "But I'm still young, I don't need to death clean now," or "I'm not terminally ill, so I don't need to think of death cleaning right now." Truth is that no one has to be too young to die clean and every state of health is not suitable to be suitable for cleaning your home. Cleansing up will improve your lifestyle and make your home more attractive and inviting. Take a look around your house Are there items that no longer serve you or didn't use in a many years? What is the reason you are keeping these items? Aren't they taking the space of your house? Certain items that you have in your house were probably not used for so long that you barely take note of the items. If you do not wear any of your clothing anymore due to the fact that they're no longer fitting the way you want them to, then they'll fit others. Give them away to charities. If you have books that you don't have any requirement for and you and your family don't require toss them away or throw them away. De-cluttering can be that simple. Just one step at a time. One room at a. One category at a.

4. Classify your objects and begin by cleaning the most basic items first. As you complete your cleaning in categories of items and start with the most basic items to wash You'll be more motivated to tidy up larger and more sentimental objects

when you move on. Start your cleaning by removing items that you're less connected to, like damaged hangers or nails that are not being used after which, as you are done taking them away, begin to clean up items that you feel more emotionally attached to. Continue this process until you get to the final emotional item that you have in your home, which are photographs.

5. Don't be afraid to give up objects that trigger memories. For example, presents from your parents or well-wishers. The memories and emotions that are attached to the occasions which led to the gift do not depend on you being attached to tangible items. It is important to learn how to release valuable objects knowing that no matter where they go, they'll be a source of happiness as well as create fresh memories.

6. Avoid removing everything from your "decluttering rage". It is better to hold onto those things that give you joy and peace. The Swedish method of dying cleaning encourages decluttering and saving. It is not necessary to dispose of everything because you don't want to stress those you love with the chore of cleaning after you've passed away. It is possible to keep items that make you happy to make your home and your daily life easier and less stress-inducing. If you have items that are of great value to your personal satisfaction but have very little or no worth to those you love make a trash bin and dispose of the items within the box after you have finished making use of these items. In the box, write "Throw these away" so that loved ones are aware the exact purpose of the things contained in it. If you plan to include your personal journals and letters into the box you are throwing away You can place an additional

note on the one of the sides, reading "Please dispose of this box. Don't open the contents."

7. Cleaning up after death gives you the chance to spend time with loved ones. When you are evaluating all your belongings, it's important to not just ask yourself whether you'll need to utilize the items, but also consider whether anyone else in your household would like to possess these items. The latter may not be difficult to determine. The best way to determine for the certainty that something that you have left behind has an important place in another's life is to inquire whether they would be interested in the item. When you gather your loved ones around and asking them if could use some of your belongings and you can take the chance to lead them through a memories by sharing about the history behind these items. It's a great

opportunity to spend time with your family members as you work to get rid of clutter.

Exercise

Sometimes, the clutter can be such a mess that you do not even know where to begin or from where to start. It's possible that everything is so mess down and messy that you simply surrender to the fate of nature and let it take care of by themselves. But this doesn't need to be your destiny. Here's a thorough procedure to help you get started in the process of cleaning your house immediately.

Kitchen Area

1. Remove duplicate cutleries

2. Reduce the number of knives you have

3. Eliminate excess stock

4. Reduce the amount of cups, plates pots, mugs, lids and pots.

5. Find the items you no have any use for. This includes supernumerary cooking appliances such as popcorn makers, doughnut makers, and more.

6. Get rid of unnecessary papers for example, menus from restaurants and cookbooks. They can be purchased online without any hassle.

Refrigerator

1. Get rid of expired items

2. Get rid of leftovers, drinks as well as frozen meat and other items that you do not would like to eat.

Pantry

1. Remove expired or unneeded foods from your pantry

2. Get rid of any unwanted alcohol or beverage

3. Get rid of all spices that no longer are beneficial or suitable for consumption.

Bathroom

1. Take out shampoos and conditioners that have been discontinued. Therefore, do not purchase various shampoos, except when it is required to.

2. Remove makeup kit which are not in use anymore

3. Get rid of any other cosmetics you don't need or use

4. Eliminate any creams that are not needed or unneeded.

5. Eliminate interior decoration that adds to the clutter of space.

6. Eliminate accessories for your hair that you do not use or require.

7. Remove any towels or blankets. Also, trim pillows and quilt covers. Also, wash mats, curtains and bath

Bedroom

1. Reduce the amount of fragrances, deodorants or fragrances. If they are not used, you can sell them and earn profit from the sale.

2. Get rid of interior décor you no longer want

3. Remove items under your bed

4. Think about removing the television. Is it really necessary to have the space? What is the frequency you utilize it?

5. Get rid of books that you're not currently using and then return them to the library

6. Get rid of items that do not belong, e.g. piano, guitar, drums, etc.

Wardrobe

1. Remove shoes you no longer wear or like

2. Remove old, worn belts

3. Reduce the amount of ties or jewelry and any other accessories

4. Take off clothing items that you no have any use for. Use the reverse hanger technique to discover items you do not need.

5. Take off the socks that are worn, pajamas as well as underwear

Laundry

1. Reduce the amount of clothes you have to wash. By reducing the amount of clothing items in your closet automatically lowers the quantity of laundry to complete.

2. Reduce the number of baskets you have

3. Keep a collection box for objects found in pockets

4. Get rid of laundry products you don't use or need for any reason

Rooms for children (playrooms as well as bedrooms)

1. Take out books you don't need. You could consider donating them

2. Get rid of old and unloved or unneeded toys. It is possible to sell any toys in good condition

3. Taken out stuffed animals

4. Remove board games that have missing pieces or pieces

5. Take away any unwanted artwork. You can digitize and keep copies of softcopies of several images before you decide to get rid of the rest.

6. Get rid of game consoles no longer being used

7. Remove dried pens

Garage

1. Get rid of any chemicals, like paints that are no longer required or do not use.

2. Take out useless parts of the vehicle

3. Take away papers that have outlived their use

4. Get rid of any gardening tools that you don't

5. Get rid of everything else you don't want or need

Living spaces

1. Get rid of interior decoration that is no longer adding worth to the living space you live in.

2. Reduce the amount of furniture you have

3. Take away any artwork or photos that are not used or loved anymore

4. Take off any cushions that are not needed.

5. Rugs that are out of style

Media

1. Remove all the DVD's and CD's that you do not use

2. Reduce the amount of appliances you use like televisions

3. Take away gaming consoles not being used

4. Disconnect chargers that aren't used anymore

5. Take away old computer, VCR, and cameras that you do not use

Items of sentiment

1. Take them off after digitizing them

2. Removing photos of people who whom you don't recognize

3. Get rid of damaged or low high-quality photos

4. You should get rid of any things you've been given, however, you don't care all that strongly about.

5. Remove any jewellery you don't want anymore

Office in the home

1. Get rid of books that you don't are using or need.

2. Remove magazines. If you need to, remove any sections you are still interested in to keep, then throw away all the remainder.

3. Eliminate papers that aren't needed, such as statements from banks utility bills, instructions guides, as well as old receipts.

4. Reduce the number of journals and notebooks.

5. Take sentimental objects out of their

6. Get rid of the printer along with other computer systems you do not require or use.

7. Reduce the amount of pens as well as writing tools

Chapter 3: A Note On Other Decluttering And Death Cleaning Techniques

Other Death Cleaning Methods and Techniques

The Swedish method isn't the sole method for dying cleaning that is available. There were many methods of cleaning the dead long before the Swedish death cleaning method was able to gain global recognition. The majority of these techniques are, however, not specifically designed or used for funeral cleaning techniques, but rather for routinely decluttering in the house. However, whatever the situation the methods are beneficial, and, together with the Swedish death-cleaning method they can be used on a large scale. The methods are described below, so that you are able to choose and select which to integrate into your funeral cleansing process.

Four bag Method

If you want to use the four bag method, you simply need to get four bags, labeling the bags as follows Donate, trash, RECYCLE and keep. Go to the room or area you'd like to clear and take everything out. Pick each item and evaluate its value or worth, then decide what bag to place it in. The process is very simple because every single item within an area must be placed in one of the bags. This method is extremely efficient and precise, since it applies to every object within the space to be cleaned. One of the major disadvantages to this method of decluttering is that, depending on the dimensions of the space that you're trying to clear it is possible to end up producing a huge mess cleaning everything and then do not have the time or energy to continue to declutter. If you've finally put the things in the four bags, you'll still need some work complete since you'll need carry your bags to their designated places of destination. This is probably the best method for those with plenty of time their hands and do their work without any interruptions.

20 Item Toss

A 20-item toss is another easy method of decluttering which can be utilized to clear clutter from out of the way in a short time. For this technique you should carry around a bag for each morning and pack it with 20 items you want to get out from your house. Do the same thing on the following day each day following until you've completely cleared your house of clutter. Be aware that the number 20 can only be used as an example but it can also mean thirteen 17, or any number that you feel at ease with. The method is straightforward yet effective. It also creates within you the habit of tidying up since you are doing exactly the same thing each day. But, it could possibly cost you money, since it isn't able to recycle as you grab hold of objects and then throw them away each day. Additionally, since you need to complete the specified number of items each day, you could find yourself throwing away things you'll need in order to meet the desired number. It is possible to consider this strategy if you don't have the drive to begin decluttering your living space, but you should get rid of it shortly after.

Detrash Technique

This method can be used to clear the house of things that do not contribute value to the space like old pencils, old toys paper, handouts, and others that no longer serve a purpose. This method is an easy to use, easy method for beginning your journey to declutter and get to the routine of cleaning the clutter in your house. Since the things you need to throw away do not really matter it is the most attractive of decluttering techniques since there are no difficult choices to be made. A major drawback to this strategy is that it relies on one of its advantages it is that you simply dispose of garbage; it doesn't aid in tackling other objects that aren't of any use. But, it's the best option for you when you've been nervous to step into the world of decluttering.

KonMari Method

The KonMari method is perhaps the most popular decluttering/minimalism approach in the world presently. It was created in 2014 by the Japanese professional organizer Marie Kondo, through her book The Life-Changing Magic of tidying up. The goal of KonMari is straightforward that you keep the objects which bring joy to you and remove the others. The concept of the KonMari technique is to clear the clutter according to categories, rather than take a room-by-room approach. The five categories found in KonMari include books, clothes papers, paper, miscellaneous things as well as sentimental objects. In order to start your own KonMari, start by taking all the clothing in your closet. Take out all your books. Next, you should take out your documents. After that, the other sentimental and miscellaneous objects. Take a look at every thing you've taken and consider "Does this spark joy?" If yes, then keep it in its proper place. If not, say thank you to the item for being a blessing to you for a long time and then throw it away. Make this a routine for all objects until you've successfully rid yourself of everything that doesn't bring you joy and only kept those which bring happiness. The benefits of KonMari's method are: KonMari method include:

The item could ensure your home is free of clutter for the remainder of your lives. Prior to purchasing an item, you can make use of to check the "does this spark joy?" filter to determine whether to purchase or otherwise.

The sentimental items are most difficult to get rid of out of your house. The KonMari technique makes it much easier to manage these objects.

It's easy to master and very effective.

The disadvantages of KonMari's method are: KonMari method are:

There have been arguments that the approach is brutal, as some items may not necessarily cause joy, but need to be within your house like toilet brush.

It is a great way to create an untidy mess.

The KonMari approach is probably ideal for those who have plenty of time for decluttering while avoiding distractions.

20-Minute Technique

The method is focused on completing smaller tasks of decluttering within 20 minutes. For this technique, you set the timer for 20 minutes. Then, you can complete smaller tasks to declutter by one daily. The benefit of this technique when compared to other ways of decluttering is that it conserves energy since you do not have to tackle all the cleaning it takes in one session. But, due to the duration the method can be a bit slow in doing a lot of work per each day. This strategy is ideal for tiny spaces like the kitchen or you're short on time and are unable to commit to an extensive decluttering program.

Weekend Method

It is popular, particularly among those in the middle class which is the majority of people who don't have enough time to clean their houses on a weekday. This is a good option in the event that you're able to bring your children to go invited to visit a family member or relatives' home so that they do not become a source of distraction. When you do the weekend plan it is basically everything decluttering you need to do during the weekend. Make sure you have plans on how to clean up to ensure that you don't make a mess that you aren't able to manage.

One Room at a Time Method

This is an effective method to clear your house of clutter. With this technique, you simply select a space by room and clean the area. The method can be employed in conjunction with other techniques for decluttering including the method of four bags and the 20-minute method to reach an acceptable level of clutter reduction. It's common to begin with the bedroom because your space where you sleep must be the quietest and most tranquil area in your home. In the wake of the bedroom is completed, it's recommended to concentrate your bathroom, since they're generally easy to manage. What you decide to do with your home's other areas will depend on your the individual's preferences. It is strongly recommended that you put off your garage until the end because it's typically the hardest space to clear. You can also make use of your garage as a place for temporary disposal to dispose of the stuff you take from every room.

Packing Party Method

Packing Party Packing Party is a decluttering game designed by minimalists Ryan Nicodemus and Joshua Fields to assist people in decluttering their home more efficiently and faster. The way to do this is to put all your possessions, including items like clothes, plates and more. Then, get them out as needed. Keep this going over 21 days. Then after 21 days, go through the boxes for any items that which you haven't touched at all. It is then your turn to determine which of the items you want to remain in your home and which must get rid of. It is possible to donate, trash or even sell the items that you don't want to keep. This is an excellent option to clear your residence in a relatively short amount of time. If you're the type that is still looking to tidy your home then this could be the most effective method. However this can be extremely laborious as the process of packing every item you have take up lots of time. One suggestion to consider when packing all of your possessions seems overwhelming is to only pack a small area of your home at one period of.

The Mins Game Method

It is a game that was created by minimalists. Mins Game is yet another game designed by minimalists in order in order to make the process of decluttering an easier, more enjoyable procedure to manage. The way to play it is as follows When you first begin the process of decluttering is day 1. On this day, clear out one item. Day 2: Declutter two things, then on to the next day until you reach the day 30 when you'll have to declutter 30 things. For the duration of a month it would be decluttered 465 objects. It's a good idea to get started at the beginning of a year or month. It can be made more enjoyable by taking before and after photographs and sharing photos on social media. It can be a great way to inspire you to keep engaged during the entire procedure. One benefit to this approach is that it helps keep your mind in a rhythm, beginning with just a few items to get rid of and progressing towards larger amounts. One of the major drawbacks to playing this game Mins Game, however, is that the first few days may be somewhat difficult, because you're only required to get rid of a handful of items. There is a chance that you will get rid of more items than you're required to and cause a chain to break.

The 90/90 Method

The 90/90 technique is an extremely effective method of assessing the value or value of the items that are that you have in your house, so you're much more aware of the items you want to keep, and which to get rid of. This method can help you rid your home of clutter house by removing things and then asking yourself "Have been using this item within the past 90 days? What will I do with this item within the next two months?" The answers you can provide will allow you to determine which item you think is worthwhile to keep. The test basically measures the worth of a product for a time period of six months (3 months in the past and three months in the near future) in which time frame, it's assumed the item of any significance in your house will be used. If you're having difficulty determining whether you will require something in the near in the future or not, put it aside as a 'could have value' object and keep an eye on it over the following three months. If after three months, the object is still not in usage, then you need to consider eliminating the item. The 90/90 strategy is a good one to speed up the cleaning process, by helping you to remove objects that simply 'hang around at home. But, it doesn't consider objects that will only be in usage for a brief period of time during the year like seasonal objects such as ski equipment.

The 20/20 Method

The 20/20 method can be useful to clear out items that you've stored just in case. The method is used to complement the 90/90 rule of effectiveness as well as thoroughness. The rule states that if you're stowing away an item you are thinking you may have in the future, you should ask yourself "Can I replace this item in 20 minutes for less than $20?" If you can, you should think about getting rid of that object. The downside to this approach is that, if you are constantly giving up items that you are able to repurchase at a cost of the price of $20, you might be spending a huge sum of money to buy items which you used to own.

Backwards Hanger Method

The method for decluttering could aid in reducing the clothes you own and also analyzing your clothes and what you do not. This method is to put all your items on hangers and arrange them on the back so that hanger hooks are facing towards you. After you have worn a certain thing and wash it and return it to the closet, but place the clothes facing forwards. Make a time on the calendar (it can be either in weeks' or months or even a whole calendar year). Take into consideration getting rid of any garment is in reverse when the scheduled date arrives, if it is the one you've never used during the time frame. For this to be most efficient as you can you should separate your clothes in seasonal categories. For instance, in the case of the summer season, only review items you wear in the summertime. It is possible that you won't need an outfit in summer. A backwards-facing hanger makes the process of organizing your closet easier and less stress-inducing. But it does have some disadvantages. In particular, it can only be used to review objects that fit onto a hanging rack, which requires a substantial storage space in order to be efficient.

Courtney Carver's Project 333

The project of Courtney Carver is an innovative approach to sprucing up your home. It's a capsule-style clothing challenge, which challenges you to only use 33 clothes objects. That includes clothing, jewelry and footwear, but does not include pajamas, underwear, exercise clothes, and any jewellery that you don't wear, such as the wedding ring. Once you have selected 33 pieces that allow you to effectively mix and blend, place all the other items of your clothing into a bag and then seal it. Make this model anew every 90 days. This is essentially letting you save only what you enjoy wearing, and eliminates the stress of having to look for' the right outfit everyday. But, it can be difficult to only wear 33 pieces of clothing over three months. If you're unable to reduce your wardrobe down to 33 items reduce it to a size which is acceptable for your needs, for instance 40 or 50 pieces in the first 3 months. and then work on reducing your wardrobe within the next 3 months.

What is the Swedish Way of Death Cleaning differs from other decluttering Methods

One of the major differences in the Swedish method of killing cleaning as well as other ways of decluttering lies inherent in the Swedish cleaning method in itself. Certain methods of decluttering include KonMari is that in order in order to decide what happens to the item you must consider whether the item is a source of excitement. If so, you should keep it. If the item doesn't then get rid of it. In contrast you can follow the Swedish approach to decluttering requires that you think about whether something is a source of joy for you however, you should consider whether it will make your life of relatives easier or better even in the absence of you. In this way, the decision to save or discard something will depend by the significance of the object to you and those of beloved family members. So, in this regard, the Swedish funeral cleaning process is more comprehensive and thoughtful as compared to the other.

De-cluttering techniques.

Chapter 4: Practical Tips And Tricks For Getting Your Death Cleaning Moving

Strategies to Begin the Death Cleaning Journey

If you're still getting into the routine of Swedish death-cleaning Here are some suggestions to make your clearing out your home as relaxing and easy as you can:

1. Learn your "Why": The first step in achieving an uncluttered home is understanding what causes clutter at all in the first place. It is essential to address this issue as the initial stage in the process of decluttering. There are three main categories of clutter people You probably belong to one of them. The three categories are as follows:

* The person who is too busy The people who are too distracted to look through their possessions whenever they require

these items. They find themselves buying an item several times. The result is that items begin to accumulate in the homes of their owners. Another reason people accumulate items is that they do not have any way to keep them in their homes. these items.

* A constant worry In this class, people accumulate items as they're worried they may need them later on. As they're afraid of not own the thing when they'll need it, they tend to store up things that aren't needed and cause clutter at home.

* The overloaded The overwhelmed: They don't want to live with a messy home however they're in a state of overwhelm by the thought cleaning out their homes, which is why they reside in the chaos.

If you know which category your self-defines it will help you identify the weaknesses you have and strengthen your strengths.

2. Be sure to ask yourself the right questions when you are sorting through your stuff. Everyone who has items that they don't need anymore has specific statements they make to themselves, which prevent their ability to achieve a healthy clutter-free life. These statements include, "I may need that", "I still have to go through that" as well as "Somebody could need that". These statements can be considered as a hindrance.

If you don't really use the product the item is not being used, then those objections will only serve as an obstacle to your clutter-free process. Learn to rid of yourself and your lifestyle from this limiting notions by taking a more objective look at things and in a rational manner. As you examine the items in your home consider these questions: "Do I really need this? Is it a source of security? What do my family members consider this item?"

3. You can set your timer for 10 minutes. Then, you can complete the decluttering task for 10 minutes. This will allow you to begin the task of cleaning. This is how it works:

Get two trash bags.

The trash should go in the bag you started with.

In the second bag add all of the stuff you don't use anymore your house, and want to either give away or sell to charitable organizations.

Be sure that the whole workout is only 10 minutes long.

Continue this practice the next day and every day thereafter over the course of 2 weeks. When you've completed your two-week time frame You should see an improvement in the house.

4. If you're not able to tidy your living space Don't create pile of clutter. Place things in the right areas. If you are a recipient of mail every now and then Get a basket that you can put all the mail that you get. Make other baskets for invites, cards for business as well as other kinds of handouts.

5. Set yourself up for a tidying process. It is a fact that cannot be understated. It is essential to begin the process of decluttering either earlier or later. So, when you get started earlier, less items you'll have to take care of. If you're overwhelmed by the clutter that is in your home begin with an organizing routine that will require one or two cleanings per day. This 10-minute approach is the best choice for you. Also, you could consider alternative methods of decluttering that

need little commitment. When you do the process consistently, you build momentum and, as time passes by it becomes apparent that you have the desire to take on the bigger and challenging decluttering task.

6. Determine the causes of clutter and then tackle the triggers for clutter and deal with them. Start by with folding your clothes or hanging them inside your closet instead of throwing them onto the floor.

7. A great method of organizing and changing your home and life for the rest of your life is using F.A.S.T. F.A.S.T acronym. F.A.S.T means:

F - Establish a time and time. It is essential to set the date and time so that it is compatible with your timetable as well as that of all those that is part of the cleanup. If you've chosen to involve your family members in the cleanup process, it is necessary to make their attendance obligatory.

A: Any object that was not used within the past 12 months could require to be taken away. If something has not been put to use within the past 12 months, it's likely that you will make use of it later on or will ever become so valuable that it will merit the space it occupies to your house. For help in determining whether you actually require the item, you should think about, "Have long ago did I have this item in my possession last? What time in the future am I going to utilize the item? Do I think it is worthy of the place it takes in my house?" Your answers to these questions ought to help to determine whether or not the object is kept or gets taken away. Don't forget to move objects between different areas inside your home. If you find that you no require an item anymore remove it!

S -- Stuff which doesn't belong to your home should be taken out from your house. If you have a home that is overflowing by only your belongings Imagine what having other objects in it can do to the space. If you've borrowed something you have borrowed, return them to their owner. If items belonging to your ex present in your house You may wish to contact them and ask them to take their possessions. If your children have mature and have their own home it is likely that they will take their things as well. Your home should be yours.

T - Throw away trash frequently. Make use of the trash container just like you would an animal that's always in need of food. Enjoy your use of the trash container. Make sure you use it regularly to store those things that you don't require, or items that have been unused within your house. Invigorate trashing with a "best trasher' competition at home. You can even award prizes for the person who has was the one to purge most frequently.

8. Make a change in your thinking about what's at home. There's no need to have those dishes your mother was using, simply because she also used them. There's no need to grant the space to dad's old golf clubs that you never need to use. Your home isn't an art gallery; you must learn to shed the sentimental things that you do not have a need for. There's no reason to be ashamed of selling items you've inherited. These items belong to another period and are in more favorable times. They don't define your life or giving them away doesn't make you someone who is unworthy. If an inheritance item has value and you aren't actually required to make use of it, you might consider offering it for auction. Things made from silver or gold can fetch an amount of

money on the market. They will bring in money but thankfully, the cash won't clog your house. However, there is a caveat to this rule with objects that are considered precious family treasures or a memory of a past moment in time. Make sure to keep them to a minimum and even create a separate area of the house for them when needed.

9. Think of your belongings as objects living things. Treat them the way you would take care of your pet. Do your socks wish to be tucked into an area behind the front door? Are your clothes happy in a squalid closet on the floor? What kind of coat would feel when it was rolled on the couch? When you make your things animated and treat them as if they could "feel", you could be tempted the items better.

10. Fold your clothes in the correct way. Sure, there's an appropriate way to fold

clothing. You should fold your clothes according to a method that makes it easy to locate them and takes up less area. A common method of folding clothes is to lay the clothes flat, then stack the clothes. The experts have suggested that placing the folded clothing side-by-side on a level surface helps them to locate...and it makes them look nicer. Furthermore, if folding vertically, you're not the need to move around the clothes to choose one at the bottom.

11. It's not a useful companion for the journey to declutter. Do not begin your process of decluttering by through each word you read or bring all the memories that are associated with an item up to the surface. The trick is to deliberately shut out your eyes and thoughts in the process, paying to the goal that is at hand, which is to eliminate items you do not need. It is much easier to say than do. For help in

getting through it, consider each letter, book or other object that triggers thoughts as a distraction which must be removed. Set these things aside in the beginning and put off the items at the end.

Strategies for getting your family Participating in the Process

Cleaning up after death isn't an easy subject to discuss and even discuss. No one wants to hear that family members say they'd like to do a big clean-up before their passing. This is a delicate subject and you should use discretion, tact and sensitivity when talking with your loved ones about the subject. The conversation doesn't need to be as if you're saying "I would like to clean up before I die;" it is possible to include a bit of flavor this statement, and modify it so that it sounds more like "I like the idea of disposing of the things we no longer need from time to time." This will not only make the cleaning more manageable, but adds a feeling of the urgency. These guidelines will help you talk about the subject of funeral cleaning efficiently and easily when you are with family members.

It is important to be in charge by example.

Your family members might be learning about the concept of funeral cleaning to the very first time they have ever heard of it in their life Some might have heard about this, but viewed it as excessive, cruel and unjust while others might have heard about it and feel great about it, however didn't have the confidence, courage or the motivation to get started with the subject. It is important to be conscious of the differences regarding perceptions and opinions and base your choice upon them. The majority of people want to be seen rather than told. If you're looking to have your family join the death-cleaning boat, then you must have been doing some cleaning every now and then The benefits must be apparent to everyone. You wouldn't, for instance, cut down on chocolate due to someone telling you. But, if the individual stopped eating chocolate and then revealed regarding how much weight they shed with no chocolates you might be attracted to give it a go. If you truly want to convince them to start your cleaning journey along with you Why not begin cleaning your home before you start? Clean out your bathroom, closet or bedroom as well as your garage. If your family members see the way these rooms are looking after themselves it could make them more than willing to get involved.

Communication skills are essential.

If you're planning take on anyone from the ship, you'll be required to interact effectively with them. To be able to effectively communicate about what you expect to accomplish it is essential to understand exactly why you're taking on the job. If you are aware of the "why", you can explain to your family members and help them to understand it also. If you've had the experience of cleaning out the possessions of someone you loved and cleaning up their house following their death Talk to your family members about how stressful and incredibly frustrating it is for the two of you. Make them aware that they are likely for the same fate If you don't start cleaning up your home right now. If you've never had this incident yourself, then you might know someone who has. Find out their experience and compare the story to your own family. Make it clear how overwhelming it can be to go through things that aren't really the ones you own.

Create a plan that is effective for all

Your family needs to have their full attention and concentration on the job at hand in order for you to accomplish the job effectively and efficiently. The best way to keep your family's attention is to establish a shared purpose and inspire the members of your group to strive for this goal. This could include selling off some of the less-used things in your home to fund the cost of a trip, or making donations to those who are less fortunate and earning a family badge and allow recipients to take a trip with their family. This is a good idea for your teenagers and children. youngsters. Setting goals like this can distract you away from the reason you're cleaning your house and instead focuses on the more fun, interesting consequences of cleaning. The family will also feel more connected, as it is now partially for themselves and the outcomes of their task would directly affect their family.

Respect your family members' boundaries and treat them with respect.

Your home can be cleaned and not necessarily have to invade any other person's space or force the people to clean their own areas. If an object is seem to be of no value to your own eyes, doesn't mean it doesn't matter for your family. Try to take care of the belongings of your family members when you interact with them, because being uninformed about their rights in the house can cause harm to anyone who has a possibility of them participating to clean up. If your family has a space in the attic or basement as well as a wardrobe located in the spare room or a desk for them to place things they want and want to keep, they can have it the space they want. They can be informed regarding the need to save the clutter down and reduce it, however, don't get to the point to move their belongings your own without their permission.

The family you care for may need the help of you

Sometimes, it's difficult to acknowledge one's disappointment over the condition of their possessions. So they hide their feelings and struggle to deal with it. If you observe you have a member of your household is struggling to find their belongings or that they voice about their frustration over the state of their closet affairs...that is the ideal opportunity to move. You can offer the person a helping hand when searching for their belongings and, while talking to them, tell them the benefits of for them to not endure the stress searching for items and also why getting rid of clutter is the most effective way to get rid of them. Keep in mind that they may not like this idea initially. Do not push too much. You've already planted seeds in their heads that they will think about when they are unhappy with how things are going.

Do not start at the top.

It is best to begin at beginning at the bottom, and then work towards the top. There is no way to anticipate your family and friends to desire to let go of the most precious items they've never used right from the beginning. It can take time before they reach a stage where people no longer wish to save items simply because they are emotionally attached to the items. The process of decluttering can be described as muscles requiring training to develop it. Therefore, begin by removing the smallest items. Remove those stale toys and dolls that they do not want to keep before you get rid of the worn and uncomfortable clothes, then bag and shoes that are worn out Then duplicate the things. Start climbing the ladder until you reach up to the highest point.

Make decluttering interesting

Decluttering needn't be a chore that is boring and stressful. There are many inventive ways to make cleaning enjoyable for you as well as your loved ones. To begin, play your hand at the Mins Game or the Parking Party. It is also possible to create your own games, for instance making a "best clean of the week' challenge for a more unique flavour to the decluttering.

Once gotten, don't lose your decluttering vibe

Be sure to tidy every now and then and bring your family members to help you. Although you might be able to clean only a couple of times throughout your lifetime, make sure to tidy up each and every so often to sustain the pace and prevent the clutter from re-entering the home and your daily life. It is possible to organize cleaning times for your family after big family events like the holidays of birthdays, Christmas, anniversary or any other major events. and remove the mess associated with these events. Also, you can create your own decluttering calendar that includes a every week, bi-monthly or monthly or more in order to strengthen and exercise your muscle for decluttering and that of your entire family. When you create a plan it is important to ensure it is not in conflict with any other schedules for the purpose of optimizing the process of decluttering. A different way to contribute to the feeling of decluttering is the introduction of a family tradition by donating to a charity home such as a charity house, which removes unnecessary items as well as preventing re-cluttering. It is also possible to employ a strategy of replacement, through asking your kids to donate their games to children who are less fortunate in the event that they would like to buy new ones. You can also advise your teenagers to donate the games consoles or computers they own in the event that they wish to buy new games.

Chapter 5: How To Write A Will

A will is a process which has been mostly given to elderly or sickly people. The idea of writing a will is generally believed to be among the things people should do prior to their end their lives. It is far from what is actually the case. Numerous legal professionals have suggested anyone who owns any valuable possession that could be passed on to other people must have a will in the first place, regardless of physical condition or age. The will can be described as a legal document that specifies exactly what happens to your assets and wealth upon your death. In this context, a will is often referred to as a "last will and testament," and the person who drafts the will who's assets will be left is referred to as the testator. It is distinct than other forms of writing like journals, in that it satisfies specific legal conditions. The requirements you will have to meet in order for it to be legal and legally binding are to be dealt with in the coming days. It is possible to hire an attorney to assist you in writing your will, or in the case of straightforward circumstances you can write the will on your own. Here steps to follow when creating a will or testament.

Beginning with the Basic steps

They are preparatory steps during the process of writing a will.

It is important to choose which path you want to follow. There are usually three choices that you could choose from

Employing an attorney may want to think about this option when your asset portfolio is very complex or your circumstance may be a little difficult. An attorney's role is to evaluate and scrutinize the draft will, offer individuals (who will typically have a neutral view on your wealth) to serve as witnesses, and verify that your will complies with legally required requirements in the jurisdiction you live in. It is the most efficient choice, but also the most expensive therefore, you should analyze your situation in detail and determine if you require an attorney.

There are times when the option of employing an attorney isn't an option. In particular, wills that are not natural in their dispositions must be monitored by a lawyer. These wills with unnatural provisions include ones where the testator gives all their wealth to individuals who are not part of their families, even though their loved ones are alive. Another example is when a testator leaves all of their wealth to an individual they've not met for quite a while.

The process of writing your own will If you want to create your own will, it is essential to first understand how law in your particular state and the requirements for it. When you have the information you need, create an outline of how you will comply with the rules. Also, you must be aware that the laws can be amended at any time and you should be aware with the latest legislation prior to decide to make plans.

Making use of an online service for writing wills Third option choice is to utilize the services offered by online will writing applications. The main benefit of this type of service is the fact that it guarantees that your will is in line to the current law and laws. Additionally, it is not too cost-effective, generally at less than $150, but this is dependent on how intricate your will.

The name you choose to use must be clearly stated on your will. This will ensure that your will won't become confused with anyone other's because they have identical names as you do. The information to be included in your will must include your full address, name and date of birth as well, if you live located in a nation that has the your social security number. If your nation does not offer one, you may choose to use the number of an official ID like an ID card issued by the national government or a driver's license.

Make a formal declaration. Any legally binding will should be preceded by a statement from the testator. The declaration should be the initial paragraph of the will and it should be written with the form of: "I hereby affirm that this is my last will and testament." If your will is not containing the crucial clause, it could not have the necessary capacity to be legally binding.

Once you've made your declaration, the next item within your will needs to be a cancellation of any earlier wills that you had made. The declaration is validating your present will, and cancels any previous wills. It could take the following shape: "I hereby nullify all previous wills I may have made at any point in the past."

Write a second statement declaring the strength of your mental wellbeing. If you discover that the testator was suffering from any mental illness when they wrote their will, then the legitimacy of the will could be unquestioned. Thus, it is imperative to affirm your self-assurance with the following statement: "I hereby affirm that I am of age to make this will, and that I have soundness of mind." In addition you can also add an image of yourself writing your will to prevent any further inquiry about your mental health when you wrote the will.

It is essential to affirm that you're not writing your will under any pressure or pressure, but rather at your own initiative. It is also possible to contact your attorney to make sure that your will won't be overturned in this respect. A statement that you should include is, "This last will expresses my wishes without undue influence or duress."

If you are a member of the family (a spouse, children, or children or wards) who you would prefer to transfer a percentage or all of your wealth You must refer to them with their full names in your will. Include your children's birth dates in the declaration. In other words, you could mention the names of your spouse and two children on your will in the following manner: "I am married to the name xxxxxx, which is later known as my wife. I have children that are xxxx xxxx (January 12 1995) and the xxxxxxx (October 8th 2012).

In the will, you must state that you have the name(s) that will be the executor(s) in your will. A executor is someone who reads the deed and will ensure it is complied with. Most often, you will appoint two executors while the third one acts as a backup in the event that the first executor is unable to due to any reason, carry out the task. In general, a person who is educated in law will be preferred executor. For declaring an executor you can use the following declaration: "I hereby appoint [executor's full name] as executor for this will. If he is absence, I nominate [second executor's name in full] as an alternate executor".

The executor is given the power to perform your duties with regard to your assets, liabilities funeral rites, and other things. If necessary, you must make written statements empowering the executor to auction off the property, lease it, or even make a pledge of some of your land property and to pay your outstanding debts as well as other charges.

Distribution of your assets

Once you have created the framework in your will, the following stage is to figure out the way you would like your estate to be divided between the beneficiaries. The process of transferring your assets to beneficiaries could be a bit difficult and you should be attentive to this phase of the procedure.

Find out what you can leave to your beneficiaries legally. Contrary to what you decide to do, it may not be legally in capability to share all your belongings, because of some conditions which could have a binding effect on their distribution. Prior to preparing your distribution plan You must be sure to review any prior agreements or contracts that you've signed. Also, you must be conversant to the laws in the country you reside in and the assets that you are able to legally transfer to another person. In particular, you can't legally leave all the assets you own in a common law country of property, since the majority of them are owned by the spouse of your choice, regardless of what your will stipulates. In contrast it's possible to bequeath all assets that are in your name within the common law nation. Furthermore, ante-nuptial as well as pre-nuptial agreements and other legal contracts can decide which assets you may or should not be able to give away.

Next, you must define clearly how your wealth to be divided to the beneficiaries. The distribution must be conducted in percentages and all proportions have to be 100 . One example could include "To my daughter, xxxxxxxxxx I leave to her fifteen (fifteen) percentage.

It is also possible to specify the items you wish beneficiaries to receive. When you make a bequest to certain assets in this manner and distribute your remaining assets will not include the assets you've handed to. As an example, you could say, "To my daughter, xxxx xxxx, I bequeath my house at 45 Park Road, and to my daughter, xxx xxx, I bequeath (ten) percent of the remainder." Try to be as precise as you can when describing the items you're giving away.

Incorporate a clause describing what happens to the assets in the event that the person to whom the assets are left dies prior to your. Example "To my wife, xxxxx xxxxx, I bequeath fifty percent of my assets should she survive me; otherwise the share of xxxxx xxxxx shall pass on to my daughter, xxxx xxxx should she survive xxxxx xxxxx and myself." If you decide to transfer the shares of deceased beneficiaries to an assets pool, which will be distributed to all beneficiaries, you can state it as follows: "To my wife, xxxxx xxxxx, I bequeath fifty percent should she survive me." That is how the share of a deceased beneficiary goes back into the asset pool.

It is important to be real about the division of your possessions. Equal distribution and fairness when the transfer of your home may seem straightforward, but it's nearly impossible to accomplish. For instance, think on how you can split three electric guitars among four children who love music, or divide two cars among three children who are adults and how to equally divide your home between adults. It is important to consider the issue for a long time before making a choice that is fair to all the parties or can be more sensible and beneficial in comparison to all options.

6. If you are the parent of minor children, it is recommended to name a guardian through your will. It is possible that you have to get the approval from a friend or family person before naming them the

guardian of your children, but experts advise against it. In selecting a guardian to your kids, experts suggest that you select at least three guardians, in the order you prefer, to ensure they aren't in danger of being left without a guardian fail be able to fulfill the duty or even die.

7. It is also possible to make a bequest under a condition. You could, for instance, declare, "To my daughter, xxx xxx, I bequeath fifteen percent of my assets should she graduate from college." One cautionary note is that it is not possible to make the bequest of an asset to one person contingent upon them marrying the person you choose or the terms and conditions that apply for bequeathing assets to an individual should not violate the law.

8. It is possible to make a provision through your will, like asking what happens to your remains after you pass

away. It should state with the words "I direct that on my death, my remains shall be buried in the cemetery at 123 Park Road."

Rounding Up

Once you've completed bequeathing your estate to the beneficiary that you choose You will have to finish off the process and wrap to complete the procedure.

Sign your name to the will. Also, it should mention your name, date of signature, and your address. Every country, state, or county have their particular rules for signing. So, be certain to research the specific regulations of your state and follow the rules. What you do with your signature could affect its legality. It is generally recommended that you add your signature to each section of your will be sure to avoid adding any other writing beneath the signature. Based on the laws of your state that prohibit writing beneath the signature could be considered to be invalid and considered to be outside the will.

It is recommended that you have your will signed before two witnesses who are impartial, however it is possible to employ more or fewer than 2 witnesses. There should at a minimum a person present. The witnesses must be required to sign a declaration that you have signed your will with a clear mind in their presence. Based on the laws of your state or country witnesses could be required appear before the court in order to verify they were in your presence when you made your decision.

Find out any additional laws that might influence the distribution in your will. For instance, in the U.S., for example it is known as there is the Uniform Probate Code (UPC) is a law that regulates the disposition of property of someone who died but has no will. Be sure to make your will in accordance to the laws of your state as well as country.

Discover the strategies used by your state and nation to distribute assets within wills. This information can be obtained through the bar associations of your nation or ask the advice of an attorney. It is essential to follow this procedure since states and nations are different in terms of the disposition of estates left to the deceased. Certain regions have the assets are transferred to the heirs who inherit them while in others where the estate is redrawn back into the assets of the deceased. In the case of, for instance, if give a home to your son and the latter dies prior to the property is left to you, it could be passed to his children, or be re-incorporated to the rest of your assets, to be divided among the other (living) recipients.

Making changes to your Will

There is a chance that, after you have signed and written your will You decide to revisit and alter the will. Check out these tips to learn the best way to accomplish this.

1. It is not generally recommended to alter the terms of your will after it is executed. The will might not be legally binding should you alter it following the addition of your signature. In addition, the person that affirmed the truthfulness of your intentions did this in the moment you first created the will, not when you modified the will, so their signature could become invalid and null. Additionally, an amended will can become ambiguous and ambiguous which means it might not be able to be carried out as you intended.

2. After you've written your will, you discover that the composition of your estate alters, you should review your will in order to make these changes, or create an entirely new will.

3. It is possible to use a codicil for minor adjustments in your will. Codicils are documents that refers back to your will in the first place and states that you're altering that will and instead of writing a new will. After its creation, your document is to be affixed to the original will in all instances.

4. If you have major changes to your life for major changes, it is possible to draft an entirely new will. As an example, you may need to make a new will in the event that you had your original will written when you were younger and the arrangement of the assets you have over time, for example in the event that you've been divorced or

remarried, or if your kids have become more mature.

Keep your Will safe and secure

It is the last step of of writing your will. Making sure your will is secure is equally important as making it clear at all as it is able to be changed fraudulently. A modified will be unenforceable or execute commands that are not the ones you have. This is neither recommended.

1. Because your final will and testament is not going to be submitted to the court at the time of your death it is imperative that it is secured and secure when you're still alive. Remember that a will not found can't be submitted. Therefore, ensure that you place your will that it is easily accessible. Consider placing it in a safe at home, or an account at the bank. It is also possible to give the will to the attorney

you trust to secure it or inform them the location at home.

2. Create a duplicate of your will, and present the copy to your executor in order to have an evidence to present at court in the event of a change in the will's original form after your passing.

3. It's best to note down the precise location of your will. If you ever overlook where your will was saved, you can simply look up this note.

Chapter 6: What Is Decluttering?

In many ways, decluttering can be an uplifting experience. The process of getting rid of unnecessary "junk" that clutters your house may appear like an easement away from you. Cleaning out your home can be laborious. The manual work required is for moving, rearranging objects, rearrange things or transport items away that need to be removed. However, it requires large amounts of emotional and mental energy to create each of these tidying choices as well as sort through the thoughts of decluttering as well as "stuff" in general might cause sometimes. This can become difficult at times, specifically when you have a lot to sort through and draw the right decisions.

Why Decluttering is Important

Today, people are anxious and stressed. Yet, many do not realize the ways in which our daily routines could cause stress and anxiety. One reason is that the accumulation of clutter and disorder can trigger anxiety, which could cause the Swedish cleansing method of death as well as the minimalistic method are well-known. Also clearing out (the process of keeping objects that aren't tangible within your home) can make it easier to discover what you're seeking. In addition, it could enhance your attitude and your mental health within the following categories.

In the Office

The advantages of organizing your workspace is not a surprise given that being exposed to messy, unorganized surroundings could hinder your concentration, interest and ability to focus. Based on previous studies of functioning MRI (magnetic image processing) findings and even deplete your brain's energy. Additionally, being in an environment that is crowded has been associated with self-reported lower productivity, as well as more frequent delay, as a result of studies published in the 2017 edition of Current Psychology publication.

Incredibly, clutter and procrastination are often mutually incompatible. As an example, research from 2019 published in Environment and Behavior discovered that anxiety and procrastination in the workplace are associated with more office clutter. In a different study in 2021, published within the North American Journal of Psychology which included 88 employees who work remotely and 88 remote employees, the findings were could be applied to remote employees; it linked procrastination and hesitation with office clutter.

The effects of clutter go beyond productivity. The report published by The International Journal of Psychological Research and Reviews in 2021 found that office clutter (which includes garbage, paper and stationary) decreased work efficiency and increased the chance of exhaustion due to work, especially those in higher-ranking post.

At Home

It's not the only location where clutter could be discovered. The clutter in your home can impact your life. In a study from 2016, that was submitted to The Journal of Environmental Psychology, Clutter could negatively impact your perception of satisfaction and wellbeing. Based on the results of a poll even though "home" is often a relaxing place, clutter can reduce some of the security. Additionally, when there's a great deal of mess, people loose control over their surroundings and this can be quite uncomfortable and could cause anxiety and despair. It can also cause anxiety, stress, or depression.

In the same way, prior research looked into how family members living in Los Angeles discussed their living environment. Also, those who described their homes as less orderly were more likely to have higher levels of cortisol and an overall depressed mood during the day than those who saw their home as more tranquil and relaxing.

Benefits of Decluttering

As I started my journey to organize and tidy my home and other activities I realized that this was going to continue to be a continuous effort. I don't even think that I'll never stop doing this task. It's a continuous procedure of figuring out what's enough and what's not. I've gained a lot of knowledge about decluttering, and discovered some amazing benefits of decluttering along the way. These are the seven advantages that I've discovered through my time.

It Helps You Save Money

De-cluttering your home in a systematic manner forces you to look at your past purchases. Certain emotions which arise out of this process, such as regret and guilt, can lead people to save the things they don't need. I became more cautious when I was spending money as I went through these emotions and feelings, and finally release myself. It was not than a way to pass the time.

In the beginning at the beginning of my shopping spree, I made it so by focusing on a list and making a plan. The higher my expectations of the items that should take place in my home resulted in shopping for fewer products. It saved me time as well as resources since I didn't have to shop in a haze. In the face of my mess I made the decision to live less extravagantly. I would rather save money and put it into items that I really like and use.

It Improves Decision-making Skills

It's a real phenomenon. If you walk into the midst of a chaotic space, or even open the door of a cupboard, you feel immediately in a state of overwhelm. Being faced with so many options can make the process of choosing a dress difficult. But the process of dressing easy as I divided my closet into two pieces and kept only clothes that I liked and felt comfortable in.

There is a possibility of building an assortment that is respectful when you wash your clothing. If you're faced with a limited selection (but there are a lot of clothes you're a fan of!) This makes getting dressed for the day a lot less stressful. It is easier to make decisions about what's left and what's gone while you purge. You choose the best products as well as the process. Making these choices in advance then you'll need be able to choose fewer options as you work with the items in your home.

It Reduces Stress

It can be stressful. Based on research the clutter significantly increases female adrenaline levels higher than males. If mothers feel anxious and stressed, it may spread to others in the family.

The burden of having more things than you have room for is a source of stress both for the parents and the children. If children are required to maintain their clean rooms and yet they have many things burden them and are not prepared to succeed. There are many false notions regarding how much they will manage.

They put a lot of pressure on themselves and other members of the family in order to function with their obligations. The result is stress and tension. Cleanliness can reduce stress on family members as well as friends. Items are stored more easily.

There is a lot of junk that was cleared away The clutter is gone and you are able to relax in your living space. Are you able to imagine your home as a secure sanctuary? If there's so much debris, the place that was intended to serve as our refuge and refuge from all the chaos outside is overflowing with items that obstruct our peace we want.

It Makes Cleaning Easier

The benefit of getting rid of clutter in your home is that it takes lesser time. It doesn't mean that you won't need to perform dishes or clean up however having lesser of them means it's less likely that they'll accumulate and cause stress. Also, it's easier to tidy down when there's not as lots of stuff lying about. As an example, cleaning requires some time, especially if you need to take out a few things from the furniture before. Also, washing countertops takes a long time with a lot of things in them. Naturally, cleaning can be difficult but it'll become quicker and easier after your house has been cleared of clutter.

It Helps You Locate Items Quickly

Do you know that US citizens are estimated to spend 2.5 days per year searching for items that have disappeared? Based on the Pixie's Lost and Found Survey in 2017, Americans have spent 2.7 billion US dollars on restoring items aren't found every year. The numbers are quite alarming! It's easier to locate items after the house has been cleared. If you find items quick, you will save effort and save money by avoiding purchasing duplicates.

When decluttering their homes it is common for people to be shocked at the amount of replicas they have already for different types of items. But, if you organize in a specific category, you'll be able to determine the value of each item has and reduce it the amount accordingly. Thus, you will have less clutter and it is easier to find and access everything you own.

It Makes Maintenance Easier

A major benefit of reducing clutter is it makes you navigate your home. Making things look tidy at the conclusion of every day's work isn't easy. If you have less possessions then there's less opportunity for things to be taken from your sight. The fact that you have less possessions doesn't mean that your house remains spotless. There are times when your home can be dirty, but it's easy to get rid of. It's much easier to tidy after you've cleared the clutter. Develop a strategy for organizing which is suitable for you.

It's much easier for all to keep pace in putting things away when you create a basic functional framework that gives everything the right place. When your home is clear of clutter and organized, it becomes much easier to manage. It can make you feel more relaxed when hosting guests or family members who are arriving at last minute. A lot of people have found that removing clutter from their homes makes them more welcoming as they are not enthralled or embarrassed over the appearance of their home.

It Reduces Distractions

There are many different avenues to explore in the world of. There is something that demands our attention on every turn. Innovation is an important factor, but so is our belongings. If we are spending excessively of our valuable time organizing, cleaning and taking care of our possessions, we forget the important things.

Decluttering can be a method of clarity. It helps you understand what the main goals of your life are as well as what's irrelevant at all. What's most significant to you along with your family? Does this reflect within your home? Simplifying our lives makes us happy fathers, mothers and also members of more connected families. In reducing the amount of distractions and unnecessary things making the space to focus on the things that matter to us.

What You Should Do Before Decluttering

If you decide to get rid of clutter If you're like me, you'd prefer to start right away with get to work. While it may appear to be the right way to go about it however, I've observed that slowing down and starting this additional step may result in better results. Prior to beginning the process of decluttering it is important to understand what you want to accomplish. It can be difficult to decide what you want to do if you don't possess a mission or plan.

Define Your Objectives

If you are deciding on the goals and objectives you want to achieve when defining goals and objectives, you must consider the goals you want to achieve and the reason behind it. What are the reasons you would like to tidy up your home? What impact would having a clean living space make to you? Make time to think over your goals to have a clear idea of the goals you're trying to achieve.

Have A Clear Purpose

It is crucial to know why in ensuring you stay motivated when get tired or lose the track. There will be times where decluttering can be a challenge. Be committed to the ultimate goal to conquer the challenges. Take a look at the whole style that you want for your home when you consider your organizing targets. Choose how each room will be aesthetically pleasing and comfortable. What would you like people to be thinking about when they enter through your home?

Define Function for Each Space

Know how the space you choose to live in is going to function within the context of your lifestyle. An inviting reception area is appealing, but when you're a parent It might not be feasible for your home to become a high-end family-friendly space. Design and function should be incorporated to create spaces that work for your needs. Be creative, but remain pragmatic about your current circumstances.

Research for Ideas

Pinterest could help you discover the style you prefer before organizing. Find items that appeal to you, and then pin them. Your style needs to be evident in the things that you've pin. If you're a fan of pins that you've collected and styles, you'll differ.

The aim of this game is to let you determine how you would like the space to look and perform. If you reside in an unadorned white space and have several photos of a rustic style (elevates hand over again) You can incorporate the style by adding accessories like blankets, accents and throw pillows, in addition to others.

Don't buy this Chip & Jojo collection at Target or go to Hobby Lobby unless you've already cleaned out. At this point you'll feel enthusiastic by the look you want and how much time you'll be able to save when you keep your house clutter free.

Get a Vision Board

As a Pinterest fan and often keep photos to spark ideas however, I am also a fan of having the real-life vision board. I tear up images and phrases from magazines and place the images to white boards. If you don't like that you can use the computer-generated collage applications accessible. They will give you the visual representation of the final goal whatever the case. It is beneficial to keep the boards in a place where you can be able to see it often (wallpaper in your smartphone hanging on the walls you frequent or even). The goals and concepts you have set are constantly reaffirmed to help you stay on the right track and motivated.

Assess Your Space

If you've got a view of the room and you have a view of the room, it's important to evaluate the current state of your room with your goals for space. Consider the following exercise and visit every part of your home. Look out from the entranceway. Take note of the issues below:

* What does this room influence me?

What is then what is the current goal?

* What would I like it to be done?

* What's happened to the magnets for clutter?

* What actions should I follow to aid me in achieving my goals and plan?

It's likely that this is among the primary reasons why many of us (including me) haven't yet achieved the goals we set for ourselves. There are a variety of methods to get rid of clutter in your home however the most important thing is to alter your attitude. Prior to beginning the process of decluttering create a storyboard. Begin with a specific goal to think about and pinpointing the areas where reality isn't in line with of what you envision can be a great approach to creating the home you'll be happy in. It is important to prepare to revisit your original goals when you work through the procedure of getting rid of clutter. When the task of decluttering becomes overwhelming or difficult take a look at how you want the house to look and work.

Decluttering Techniques

You've decided to clean your living space, but where can you begin? There are a variety of methods to getting rid of clutter. Let me go over a few of them in order to help you in figuring out a method to declutter your home. What's the best place to start? If you're overwhelmed with the amount of stuff that are in your home, setting to clean up could be one of the toughest parts. Think about the following things:

Are there any places you can easily clear that could have a significant impact?

Which areas in your home seem to be prone to accumulation of the most often?

* Which section or room of your house gives you most anxiety?

The responses you provide will help in determining a plan for decluttering. Begin with a place that it is easy to clear however leave an impression. My personal preference is my kitchen counters (which could be my solution to the second question). There are many ways to go about cleaning out your kitchen. Let me talk about four. Take note of what you think could work to your home as well as you while you work through each day.

Best decluttering techniques include:

KonMari by Marie Kondo

If you are decluttering, Marie Kondo recommends removing anything with a similar design. In the case of getting rid of your wardrobe then you'll have to get rid of the entirety of your clothes. This means emptying out your storage space, linen closet or any other place that you've kept clothing within your home. The process could be difficult for certain groups because it is possible that we don't know what the exact location of each office item within the home is stored.

Being aware of the things you've got

One of the main reasons people accumulate many things is that they're not always aware of the quantity they accumulate. The size of their homes is higher by a wide margin which gives them more space to spread their belongings. In the event that goods are kept across multiple locations, they end up having doubles as well as unfinished items. It's enlightening and instructive to take everything in one place in one go to review and see what's left and what is left. This is an essential stage in the process because it lets you decide exactly what you would like to keep or dispose of. The Marie Kondo method Kondo process creates an underlying sense of belonging, that makes it much easier to prevent bringing clutter back within the home.

The 20-Minute Method

The method of decluttering is the setting of a timer to run for 20 minutes, and completing tasks in small chunks of time. This has the advantage it is less prone to become exhausted or exhausted within a 20-minute time frame. It is a disadvantage that you will not be able to cover an extensive space in such a small duration. It is a great option for smaller, less defined areas, such as kitchens (1 cupboard or drawer at a given time). The idea may not work efficiently in a closet in the absence of specific pieces. If you're on a tight budget yet still want to make some progress, this approach works best. If you follow this 20 minute routine every day and you'll complete a large amount of work.

Weekend Plan

This article is targeted at the person willing to start the process of removing clutter and sanitize at the same time. It is a great thing for being incredibly determined and are able to find someone who will take care of your kids during time you are working while you revamp your house and work on every section.

The speed of decluttering can be compared to racing an entire marathon. However, it is effective for a certain group of people. If you decide to adopt this method create a strategy for how you'll take care of the rooms. It's not a pleasant feeling having completed each part of the home, and then realize that you've ran out of time and energy to finish each one.

One room at a

The method of decluttering one room at a go is straightforward to comprehend. Start with one area and then move through the house by room. If you follow this method, start by cleaning the room you are able to tidy and move towards the more difficult places to clean.

* Bedrooms: It's important to clean your bedroom prior to beginning the course of exercise. Your bedroom is where you sleep and is the one that should be tranquil and relaxing. There's no peace or relaxation when the only thing you look at before heading down the stairs in the evening is books, clothes, or other odd things piled up in your bedside drawers or tables.

Bathrooms: Toilets are a great early-on task since they're usually relatively easy since the majority of people do not have any particular attachments to bathroom items.

Other rooms There is no limit for you to decide how to organize the different areas of your house. Some rooms are larger or contain more objects so they'll take much longer. The rooms could be rearranged in segments.

* Objects with a sentimental meaning The room I'm recommending finishing is the toughest room that usually houses the most sentimental items. Garages are the last space. It's advantageous make use of the basement production space, while also working at other rooms in your house. It is possible to store things for a short time until they can be offered for sale or donated

No matter what method you decide to take for cleaning, it is important to consider these tips before you begin.

- Evaluate your personality

* Time availability

* Space is free

* Items of personal value

* Attitude

Various decluttering strategies suit different folks. There is no one size fits all approach, and a variety of decluttering methods may work in different situations. The entire house on a single weekend may be enough for most. However, some people have the capacity, desire and motivation to accomplish that, and it's the best approach.

If you're struggling with it and find it difficult to purge your home it is recommended to start with smaller spaces and shorter durations of duration.

The process becomes more manageable as you progress, however it's important to begin with an environment that won't overpower you. Limit the scope of your work so that they are completed. At some point, you'll be prepared for the next project.

* Time available: There is nothing more frustrating than starting a project only to finish it half way through then needing to end it because there's no time left to complete it. If you are aware that it is going to become a bigger undertaking and can accept the idea of abandoning the project to revisit it at a later time, that's acceptable. Make sure your schedule will allow you to finish the work in a sufficient amount of time. In all ways of cleaning clutter, it's likely to increase prior to getting better, so abandoning the task midway through could feel a bit deflating. Opt not to begin more

substantial projects if you're running to time.

* Space: Prior to you begin one of these methods to declutter examine the area you are living in. Make sure you and the family are prepared mentally to allow the space to become chaotic as you work across the area. It is recommended to work in only one room at a period of time. It's stressful to find every room chaotic. Most people do not like having to deal with incomplete projects. Examine how the development of your space will impact the efficiency of your home and the family members during this time. In the case of, say, if you plan to cook the dinner, which involves lots of preparation work during the day, it may be a bad time to get rid of your entire kitchen.

Do you have a collection of belongings? Have started decluttering your home and only discover that fifty percent of your belongings do not belong? It's okay to focus only on you and your things, but don't think of working on all the rooms alone after you've had a discussion with your partner, and they've allowed the freedom to eliminate whatever you like (most people don't).

Set these dates so that your partners and you cooperate. The materials you can throw away and have your partner review them. But, it can be a bit tense if looking at all the things you are being taken away and your partner is refusing to give up any of the items. Be aware that you can just control your behaviour as well as your belongings. Be respectful of each other's belongings and emotions. Discuss and work as efficiently as you can.

Process of Decluttering

It is recommended to have four containers or boxes for each of the options for decluttering that include one for garbage and one for donations and one to sell (recommended) in addition to another for your own space. Think about the following four important concerns:

1. Are I using and enjoying this product?

2. Do I want to purchase this product today?

3. What else do I can use to perform exactly the same job?

4. Do I really will require in my in the near future?

A good answer can assist you to determine the things you would like to keep and what you'd like to get rid of. It is your responsibility to control the quantity of clutter that is within your home. When you get more comfortable and make decisions, it becomes easier. When you're stuck, place it in a possible pile then return once you've gone through everything else. If you're unsure about it about letting the item to go, secure it in a secure place with a date for expiration in it. If you've never missed something until the time that day is upon us, don't hesitate to share.

Things for sale

If you find yourself with lots of goods to offer, you must take caution. Selling things takes time and experience. This can take more effort than worth it, particularly when you've never tried previously. Also, you may realize that your items are more valued than you anticipated.

You must set a deadline for when the items must be sold, if you want to offer them for sale. If they aren't being in use by that time, you can offer the items to your relatives, or a local purchase, organisation, or donate them.

Marketplaces and Facebook groups and 'Offer Up I have had the most effective result. I've always utilized eBay however I've stopped as they are now charging trading fees. If you're selling items take care about the details you give to people and how you interact to them.

Keep your focus

All of these organizing strategies may appear to be something to do. It's hard to begin however once you've done it, you'll be happy that you took the time to do it after seeing the way you feel. Maximize the successes you have had and push ahead. There will be some tasks that are harder than other, but you must keep going and never give up! You will reap the rewards when you are more free and relaxed. Break down large tasks into manageable tasks and keep doing these. If you need additional assistance or motivation, ask for the help of a coworker or consider hiring an organizer. While you're working, take photos before and after. In times of exhaustion, they may inspire you to continue moving forward.

Be sure of the goals you want to achieve.

Review your goals and plan as well as remember the reason you started decluttering in the initial time. An additional quick victory could help you to regain your timetable.

Make sure your space is clutter-free

Whichever method you choose in decluttering, you'll have to establish a strategy for managing your clutter to follow. Take these steps for keeping your clutter in check.

Change your settings

Use the guideline of one minute

Be cautious when purchasing products.

• join a supportive group

Changes in the system: Disorganization is often caused by the insufficiently organized environment which is suitable to how you will use the space. When these processes are implemented, the objects will be placed back where they belong once you're done the process of removing the task. If the items you have aren't in a location find one in line with the manner your home is run.

The one-minute rule: Follow the 1-minute rule. If it takes less than one minute to put something away and return it straight away. Make a container ready for items that should be stored to other places for things that take more time. You can fill the basket every day, or at least once and put the items back in their appropriate locations.

Make sure you are cautious before making purchases Be modest: Living in a modern society requires an arduous commitment. When you purchase an item, ask yourself if you really need or want the item. Be deliberate in your buying. The purchase will not be a mess even if you haven't bought it in the first place. Try your best when purchasing products, and stay away from purchasing impulsively. You can opt out of mailings, newsletters, as well as promotional emails to limit the marketing messages you receive.

Chapter 7: Swedish Death Cleaning

Swedish Death cleaning the process of organizing and clearing the house prior to your passing so that you can ease the burden on family members after your death. Swedish funeral cleaning is usually carried out by older people or sufferers of an illness that is terminal.

Even though Swedish Death Cleaning could be thought of as a horrifying crime scene cleaning however, it's really a practical and effective way to get rid of clutter. Yes, this may be a little morbid. But, Swedish Death Cleaning might offer some advantages immediately, as it helps you identify what items are really valuable and those you're ready to dispose of. Think of it as an Scandinavian twist on The Konmari Technique, instead of being a sad end-of-life task.

The Origin of Swedish Death Cleaning

The term 'Swedish Death Cleaning is a term coined by author Margareta Magnussen, who wrote the publication The Gentle Art of Swedish death Cleaning and How to Free your family and yourself from an entire lifetime of clutter. Magnussen encourages readers to think about the relatives who have to sort through their possessions following their death as well as tips for making their job the simplest task feasible.

Practically, it means cleaning and organizing your house in order to reduce the stress in sorting through a myriad of things and then determining which are crucial. Then you'll be able to accomplish the job for them by using Swedish Death Cleaning, by only keeping items that you consider to be essential.

"Oftentimes you truly discover you can't shut your cabinets or closing your room door," notes Magnussen. "Whenever that occurs, it is unquestionably time to act, when you're only in your forties." In the event that you're further years away past death, you could refer to this cleansing as dostadning." This is referred to as dostadning in Swede that is one of two words "do" (which is a sign of death) as well as "standing" (which is a sign of the cleanliness) according to the information she provides in her book.

Magnusson is a native of Sweden and is believed as "between the ages of 80 and 100." While she's lived in various countries, she is now in a 2-room apartment located in Stockholm, Sweden. She has cleared out the homes of relatives, friends and coworkers in addition to her home where she resided in with her partner following his passing. While the Swede stresses the benefits of a post-death homekeeping publication, she also stresses that it's also about performing the right thing for those who live beyond your lifetime.

How Does Swedish Death Cleaning Work

Though Magnusson's target audience is typically adults above the age of 50 however, she insists it applies to anyone seeking an unhurried and fulfilling life (which suggests it's almost universally applicable to everyone). It's not so much to begin contemplating your mortality, but rather to change your mindset towards collecting more and more things each year. Magnusson's thoughts contain the flavor of Swedish simplicities, and it can resonate with adult from any age.

Be calm You don't need to be a maniacal housekeeper to implement this technique. "Death cleaning doesn't mean cleaning up and dusting the mess,' Magnusson explained to The Chronicle.

It's about a longer-term sort of organizing that lets the daily routine run quickly.'

Magnusson's strategy is in stark contrast to the steamrolling method of swiftly clearing your house of all objects. But it's a process that could last for many months and even years, if needed and the end outcome should be a lasting change in the way you organize your house and family instead of sporadic bursts of decluttering, accompanied by further purchase of things you'll not ever need.

As you are rearranging your items You may need get started in preservation containers or bags and label the boxes based on what you intend to do with them or give away their belongings.

Before you begin SDC make sure to consult family members close to you.

This isn't something that can be accomplished by yourself. It is important to communicate your goals to those you love in an easy and clear approach, while stressing that the intention was to make everyone's lives easier and more peaceful. You may find them to respond strongly and need to adjust and keep by highlighting the benefits of an easier, more tranquil life while everyone is present, and not worrying about somebody they cherish dying.

Start by asking them to give honest feedback regarding your possessions. Will you keep the equipment it wasn't for the owner? Are they interested in the treasures of your tea cups, coins as well as porcelain models? If they don't require your items and you're ready to let them go offer it to them or even sell it via Ebay.

How Swedish Death Cleaning Can Change Your Life

The earlier you rid yourself of unnecessary things from your life, the better. It's likely that you've heard of eliminating things that do not make you feel happy as an identical process.

Swedish Death Cleaning is a way to encourage people to look at what you aren't using. This method assists in making your home more organized and makes it easier and more enjoyable. It is a way to clear mental and emotional clarity and eliminating waste. Death Cleaning helps you to the determination of what is truly precious to you. Additionally, it helps reduce stress as having less things to worry about means less stress.

The element of nostalgia is one of the most important aspects of death

Cleaning. If you are able to simplify your lifestyle it gives you the chance to think about why particular things are important for your life. This helps you reflect about the past, while acknowledging the abundance you enjoy today.

The overall learning process will teach that joy comes from relationships, not items. The material items can make people feel content for a few minutes, however, that feeling is only fleeting. The desire to buy another item to feel good afterwards but this could get into a flurry. A desire to purchase further "things" just makes you anxious and depressed. I decided to try Death Cleaning, and then it increased my energy and motivation. It's extremely purifying. It makes you to feel extremely productive and can even inspire you to perform other things.

They can also help your mental well-being. Accepting the fact that you are dying, however dark as it might be could give you a greater perception of your self. The acknowledgment gives you an understanding of what people might think about your character. It will help in understanding the way you want to be appreciated and viewed now and in the near future.

Swedish Death Cleaning involves more than just organizing your workspace. It's about digging deeper, and using your judgment to remove unnecessary items you don't require. It is important to not tackle many things at a time. If you are trying to complete all of it at the same time- - and then completely rebuild your life, you'll be unhappy and disappointed. Start with a small amount and begin to work up.

It is important to note that you should avoid starting with personal items and pictures. First, you must build up the ability to manage emotions that come with this task by tackling other tasks without a heavy emotional burden.

The closet can be a great location to begin (however I, personally, I started with my car). Things that aren't needed can often be stored in closets. It will help you prepare to tackle a larger task like a room for storage. Then move on for larger tasks such as the bedroom. After that, move on to the sitting room, etc.

Tips for Following the Swedish Death Cleaning Method

Swedish death-cleansing is in part focused on determining what you do not want anymore. While death cleansing is a method of to prepare for the inevitable future, the author emphasizes the importance of striving to make your life more comfortable and productive today. These tips for death cleaning can also be helpful for cleaning your home.

Step 1: Decide When to Start

According to Magnusson the age of 65 is the ideal age at which for beginning the cleansing process. It is important to have the technical ability perform the task, and also have some time. There are a variety of indicators of when you should start cleaning. It's crucial to start decluttering when you are unable to shut a cabinet or put an item in the closet or you are grateful someone has a plan since you weren't able to decorate your home.

Step 2: Start with Simple Activities

As the possibility of immediate success is inspiring, you should make your first journey into dying as straightforward as is possible. Magnusson recommends starting with large objects that have no value like furniture, then moving on to smaller things that are sentimental like photographs. An entire decade of personal interaction can be more time-consuming and difficult to study in the same way, so you shouldn't wish to feel overwhelmed by the feeling or a plethora of items you have to deal with right away. Instead, tackling objects that aren't being used or stored, as an example is an opportunity to win. Magnusson is the one who initiated the method, typically starts with clothing since you almost always are carrying more than you require. Also, it's quite easy to give them away in the case that someone dies and needs cleaning.

Step 3: Identify What to Throw Out

The main objective of Swedish cleansing of the dead is to clear the mess. Follow these guidelines to decide what should remain as well as what can go

• Assess abundance: cutting out the excess food is an essential idea. Keep dishware in line with the number of people you're able to accommodate in the area you live in such as. The catering for 12 guests is not necessary for a home that can have only eight people. Consider these 11 things in your wardrobe you ought to get rid of.

Do you need to assess the importance of something you believed that you had or are unable to remember the name of it or where it came from? Do you really walk through something but have not noticed the item? Be sure to say goodbye if it's value has diminished. "Will this make someone happy if I keep it?" This is a simple but effective way to assess the quantity you've got. If the answer is yes, it could be ideal to give it with someone right away instead of storing it for handling it in the future.

Step 4: Seek Assistance

Simply letting people know that you're dying clean (or cleaning out) isn't just helping in a sense of responsibility, but is an excellent method to invite others know that you can help or ask for items that are worth looking at. If you're looking for help, Magnusson firmly believes in adhering to the timetables of other. Make sure you have precise questions as well as photos of the items that you're seeking to do physical work, or contacting an acquaintance if you want specific tools, or obtaining an evaluation from a library.

Step 5: Let Go of Unnecessary Stuff

Reselling, giving to charities or removing objects after Swedish funeral cleaning are among the well-known methods for disposing of objects. Magnusson states that it is common to have issues with giving to charities, so make sure you do your research before you give your gift away.

Giving away is a way to save sentimental items aren't yours but that you can't think of seeing be donated to a charity. The mother-in-law of Magnusson gradually piled presents on her family. Grandma could not only be adept at connecting with her family through a variety of gifts while she lived and working, it also made sure that, when she finally downsized her home, she been able to get rid of a number of items.

But, Magnusson warns against recommending items that don't fit the person's personality or culture. Make sure you are thoughtful when giving gifts Also, don't get at all if someone says"no" or refuse to accept something.

Step 6: Preserve What Is Most Important

It is the "throw away" container is crucial for a proper Swedish funeral cleaning. When you think, "Would somebody be pleased if I retain this?" Remember that it could be someone the person you are. It is the best place to save personal possessions which are only valuable to you, and you would like to save, and letting everyone know (or anyone who might be people who could be) to be donated with no shame or resistance.

Other Traditional Methods of Cleaning Similar to Swedish Death Cleaning

KonMari Method

KonMari Technique KonMari Technique is pro-organizer Marie Kondo's method of arranging your stuff by categories, instead of by space. The KonMari Theory's aim is to build a house filled with things that make people feel content. Although many associate her method of housekeeping as a way to improve their lives, it's actually focused on getting rid of things that no longer serves you. Kondo advises to begin by getting rid of all items from your closet and cabinet (category one) as well as all books on your shelves (category 2.) as well as all paperwork from your desk and storage containers (category 3).

If you've got a huge pile of stuff, go through it one by one and determine what makes you smile. Even though Kondo acknowledges that this could be a bit odd or strange at first, she reminds people who follow her that you'll become more adept at identifying the things that make you happy when you move. When you've cleared out things from each group and you'll be able to have a much smaller number of items to put back into different cabinets, closets bookcases, and other containers. Keep in mind that you have to finish one section before moving on into the subsequent.

Feng Shui

In fact, feng Shui is a style that places less focus on clearing clutter and more emphasis on the way things are placed. The feng shui method is often straightforward and easy to follow, which can be attributed to a lot with the way that energy is able to flow through an area.

Feng Shui is a traditional Chinese tradition that influences everything from design to the arrangement of one's personal space. Feng shui is a method of bringing your environment in line to the flow of nature in the universe by paying attention to the cardinal locations (such like West as well as South) in addition to organic elements like wood and metal.

It is similar to Taoism and is based upon living in harmony with the flow of energy or Qi with its various expressions as well as natural rhythms. Yang and yin are two opposing energies, which are different forms of 'qi'. Feng Shui emphasizes harmony between the components and energies.

It is suggested that those seeking to get a relationship give space for the person by setting up their furniture in groups (such for their bedsides tables) as well as having the bed accessible on either side. If you want to have a successful experience in your workplace, place your desk in the best place -- or the position where you will be able to be able to see your entire home.

Hygge

Danish Hygge is all about being kind, and when we stop paying attention to our surroundings, chaos begins to take over our lives as Hygge is no longer achievable. The clutter creeps in at a sly pace and without notice. It pops up out of thin air and immediately takes over your daily life. It is the goal of building an area that is conducive to wellbeing and clutter-free A home that is designed to assist you to build the Danish Hygge environment and lead an environment that is more flexible.

Hygge could refer to various aspects of life, one of the most common uses is with regards to the decor of your home. Because a lot of the stuff that keeps us comfy and secure is a result of the interior of our homes, it's not a reason to be surprised that it's commonly associated with interior decorating.

Lagom Concept

Lagom is a philosophical method that originates from Sweden which is generally effective in homes as it is be in many other areas of life. Lagom (voiced in the form of "lah-gum") is a Swedish word that literally translates into "just enough." This is a notion that encourages moderation across all aspects that are involved in daily life. It's based upon the belief it is important to balance your life. path to happiness.

Even though lagom doesn't add much to homes, its mentality is a key factor in the cozy minimalist style of Scandinavian interiors. Lagom homes are situated between minimalism and maximalism, with just enough' of the things we cherish to make us feel relaxed and content.

Chapter 8: Benefits Of Swedish Death Cleaning

Although the aim is to lessen the stress for your family and friends after your passing, Swedish death Cleaning provides other benefits. This is something I'd like to investigate next.

Fewer Material Creates Little Clutter

Doing your best to clear out rubbish means that there is less mess in your home. It's easier to keep your home clean and housekeeping will be easy. One of the main benefits that comes with cleaning your home early in the day. In the event that you live on a smaller budget, you will enjoy a better quality of life. The removal of items isn't an everyday task for cleaning. This isn't the right way to go if you need to clear your countertops of kitchen dishes, mail food items, cups as well as other things prior to attempting to organize. Get rid of clutter and you'll realize that you've got plenty of storage space to store things you want to keep. Living with a small space makes you appreciate what you own.

Discover Your Necessary Items

It is common to be surrounded by much more stuff than we actually need. If you make the effort to reduce clutter and only keep just what you require then you'll gain an improved knowledge of the things you own. This will leave you feeling happier and even more content. You are aware of everything you require and do not need more. Find out the main causes behind clutter, as well as how to eliminate it permanently.

Greater Adaptability

It happens, and you're required to perform an 180-degree pivot in a hurry like when you have to move immediately. You'll be more flexible when you're less cluttered. There is no need to think about how you do with large amounts of rubbish. All you need is to take your essentials, and go.

Help to ease the load of work from family As well as Friends

In the past that the primary goal of Swedish death Cleaning is to avoid leaving the family members of yours to tidy up after yourself. Start with items you've hidden in places such as the basement. It is your opportunity to eliminate items which could be harmful or embarrassing for family members to find. If you know the way you want your belongings to be treated after the passing of your loved ones, this could be the perfect time to write an announcement or send a message to anyone. Also, it relieves them of having to figure out what to do with the items you have. If people ask the provision of specific items to them. This way, you'll make sure that the items will be delivered to the right homes. You shouldn't assume that customers are interested in your product.

Discover Your Keepsakes

Margareta Magnusson's novel The Gentle Art of Swedish Death Cleaning: How to Get Yourself and Your Family Free From a Lifetime of Chaos is among the most well-known books about the topic. It is recommended to save memories for the end since decluttering items that are emotionally charged could cause you to go down a path. It is possible to get so caught up in reminiscing about the past that you put off clean-up. Create your own "Throwaway box." It is simply a container filled with objects that matter for you, but may not mean much to other people like photographs or love letters.

Swedish Death Cleaning that you could do in your own way. It's not necessary to be ahead of the game - only items you're not using or care about. This, as well as the other steps, eases the stress on your loved ones after your passing. Most importantly, it improves the quality of your living as well as allows you to enjoy your possessions while living. In light of this obvious fact and ultimate goal this technique may not work ideal for everybody, but it's really not all that different from normal clearing out.

Chapter 9: Some Myths On Decluttering

There are many misconceptions concerning how to lead an orderly and normal lifestyle. The popularity of Marie Kondo's work The life-changing magic of tidying up and the Japanese Art of Decluttering and Organizing seems to have muddled these concepts even more regarding the concept of clutter. In the book Marie Kondo, the Japanese organizing expert shares unusual ideas for decluttering. Her name is well-known for her admonishing that anything your possessions do not "spark joy" inside you is to be removed from your home.

Seven myths regarding Decluttering and the truth about it

There are many methods of cleaning and organizing your space. Techniques and methods of decluttering that are successful only for a particular person won't be a success for all. We'll review seven cluttering myths, and the truth that lies behind their underlying causes.

Assumption #1: You have to remain in order all the time

The truth is that accumulating the accumulation of clutter (even only on a tiny scale) is a natural part of life, regardless of the level of cleanliness you have. The idea of being organized all the time isn't feasible or practical.

Sometimes, after a lengthy and busy day, you just want to relax rather than take care of cleaning. It's fine, there's it's not a problem. Give yourself a little space and try to get your house clean on the following day. Your brain will feel refreshed and you'll likely work more quickly and efficient in organizing your tasks.

The aim is to establish the timetable and a routine which will help you clean your home and not be overwhelmed or stressed due to the need to clean. In reality, unrealistically high expectations about organization will cause anger and disappointment.

The second assumption is that decluttering should only be done once the course of.

Reality #2: Decluttering should be an ongoing process.

Spending hours in the task of decluttering is a great way to get rid of the overwhelming, chaotic feeling that makes it difficult to live in an overcrowded home. Making a decision to eliminate clutter is an excellent first move, but it's all it takes. An annual decluttering program that is focused simply won't be sufficient. Decluttering every day is the ideal option to make sure your home stays always neat and tidy. Make sure you set an aside each week for complete this task. Give a few extra minutes to the decluttering or organizing tasks at least once per time throughout the year.

Assumption #3: Space that is free is not healthy.

Truth #3: When it comes to the visual appeal the space can give an impression, the majority of times it's all about what's missing.

The derogatory nature of the word "empty" contributes to the impression that blank spaces are an undesirable thing. Interior designers often take a phrase from the art marketplace to refer to areas of the home that have been deliberately not occupied with furniture or artworks in the walls are referred to in the form of "negative space." There's no reason to be surprised that this idea has earned a negative reputation and the term "negative" is pretty simple to grasp.

Decluttering goes beyond cleaning and getting rid of all the mess. It could even be a deliberate design decision that keeps the space (or spaces) not occupied. This can accomplish two goals. In the first place, a less "busy" environment can be peaceful and more soothing to our minds. The absence of empty spaces can allow various aspects of the room to be drawn out and attract our focus.

Assumption #4: A minimalist life is the ideal way to go.

The reality is that it's not for everybody.

One of the most common misconceptions about decluttering is

that minimalist living is ideal for everybody. The work of Magnussen and the other news stories that urge us to rethink our excessive consumerism have inspired more and more people to discover ways to manage their lives with fewer items. However, dramatically expanding and shrinking within a tiny condo, home, or a 200 square feet of a containers isn't a good idea ideal for all.

Possessing more things than what you actually need will make you a less privileged person than a person who has simply. This is merely a matter of your personal preference. Try to avoid going overboard with your purchases until you're overwhelmed by the clutter. "Control your things, don't let your things control you," according to the saying is said.

The assumption #5 is that a disorganized individual is not able to alter their poor organization habits.

Truth #5: This is one of the myths we need to declutter which we completely dismiss.

The ability to be organized is a gift and not an individual quality. Like every other skill that can be learned and developed over experience. The key is the determination of a person and their patience when it comes to developing this talent. It is true that trying to convince an elderly family member who's been chaotic for all their lives to abruptly alter their behavior and turn into somewhat of a control individual will take a lot of effort.

Complete the gaps with any phrase you want to use... "An old dog can't learn new tricks," "a leopard can't change its spots," and etc. But we are able to modify. Also, we can alter idioms such as "if you're not learning, you're dying," "if you're not learning, you're not developing," and "if you're not learning, you're not living" (along with a myriad of other pearls of wisdom on the process of learning) are not true.

Assumption #6: Individuals who tend to be chaotic may be able to organize themselves without help.

Truth #6: There are a variety of great organizational tools available. Use them, especially if you are having difficulty staying organised.

One of the biggest decluttering pitfalls is that you could make your house tidy and neat, without engaging with great organization and storage methods. Yes, it's feasible however, why should it be nearly impossible? There are many great solutions readily available, like bedspreads and closet organizers specifically designed to improve storage space as well as save time in order to stay organized. They might not do all the work for you in regard to organization however they can simplify the process.

7. It's possible to manage the clutter.

Truth #7: It's really possible to lead an unorganized life, and simply adapt to the chaos which surrounds you. Unfortunately, the longer you don't take your time with mess, the more chaotic your life will get.

Take a look at how much energy you use every day to search for things in your apartment or home that is not organized. Based on a poll conducted recently, the average American is spending 2.5 days a year searching for items that have gone missing. It was estimated that the average time spent looking for one lost item exceeded five and a half mins.

In addition to the waste of time created by clutter experts in medicine know for a long time that an excessive amount of clutter can cause insomnia, stress as well as other health issues. Do not be deceived by many decluttering myths in the market. It is true that every person needs help from time to the time to keep the cleanliness of their home and lives. The concept behind Structured Interiors will assist our clients to make room to live in rather than just surviving with the mess of their homes.

Chapter 10: Sustaining A Decluttered Environment

After you've cleaned out your home and are ready to leave it in a clean and tidy state so that you don't have to do it once more. Put bins close to places where clutter tends to build up so it is possible to collect items for recycling, even if you're tired or in a rush. You can, for instance, keep in a bin or box:

* To take out empty rolls of toilet paper Stop by the toilet.

* Gather containers, cans, glasses and other containers to store within the kitchen. (Note that bags for carrying can be reused in specific areas when you use the bags.) Pick a different kind of bag, if the ones you have can't be reused.

* To dispose of garbage paper in front of a desk

To collect newspapers and magazines take a seat on your comfortable seat.

* Collecting ink cartridges that have been discarded on the computer's desktop

Place your table near the post box for collecting mail (to reduce clutter and prevent the loss of an important characteristic)

There are a few ways you can ensure that your home is clutter-free.

Cultivate a Minimalistic Way of Life

If you have a continuous stream of items entering the home, there must to be a continuous stream of stuff leaving your residence. If this equilibrium is not maintained, then clutter is likely to develop. If you're constantly creating new items for your house, you might consider incorporating a bit of minimalistic habits into your daily routine. It will not only reduce the chaos, but also help conserve money. For resolving a problem with clutter it is not necessary to go through the process of becoming a strict minimalist however, eliminating unnecessary items in your home and delaying the return of these items can be helpful.

Giveaway Something Old Once You Purchase Something New

Apart from food items medicines, utility bills and cleaning products, as well as basic items, and clothes particularly important, you should try to either recycle or offer another item every time you are bringing something to your home. Your item to be thrown away should be the same as the bought one. You could consider using an old newspaper to recycle it before buying a new one. Better yet, give the magazine to someone else in order to let them appreciate it. You can also borrow magazines from libraries instead of buying them, or read their digital versions if you can.

Consider your purchasing decisions Be sure to consider your buying decisions

It is a good idea to look at your purchase and figure out what percentage they are really needed. If something needs to be used for the protection of either animals or human beings and animals, then it has to be bought. Things that provide enjoyment as well as allow rest are also essential. You may also be surprised at the number of items you are able to steer clear of.

Minimize Paper by Going Online

Internet connectivity has many benefits in the fight to reduce the amount of clutter.

* Newspapers and magazines online If you have an electronic device, you can join digital versions of newspapers and magazines rather instead of purchasing printed copies. If your library is signed up with them it is possible that you will be capable to read them for free fee.

* eBooks: If you can get a discount or free ebook can be found, think about giving away or resending the book in its printed version. If you can, buy electronic books or use online access instead of paper-based books. To ensure that your ebooks are not lost keep backups of them in different areas.

* Internet bills: A variety of bills are able to be dealt with electronically, and a lot of applications can be done on the web,

removing the requirement for printing versions of paperwork. Security is, however, a crucial aspect in these actions. If you do not receive regular reminders in your mailer, you need to ensure that you pay your bills in the due date. Certain companies send out email reminders however, not every one.

Recycle Your Paper Articles

Many free newspaper waste, flyers, and other items were sent to my home. They pile up quickly and are one of the biggest kinds of junk, especially when the covers of magazines are damaged and thrown away by my pets. In the event that new or updated fliers and local papers are released to me, I create an habit of throwing away the outdated copies, regardless of whether they're never read--no exceptions. They are also available online for readers to access.